MIND BENDERS

GAMES OF SHAPE

IVAN MOSCOVICH

Vintage Books
A Division of Random House
NEW YORK

A VINTAGE ORIGINAL, September 1986
FIRST EDITION

Original concepts copyright © Ivan Moscovich 1986
Text and illustrations copyright © Eddison/Sadd Editions Limited 1986
All rights reserved under International and Pan-American
Copyright Conventions
Published in the United States by Random House, Inc., New York,
and simultaneously in Canada by Random House of Canada Limited,
Toronto

Library of Congress Cataloguing-in-Publication Data

Moscovich, Ivan.
    Mind benders : games of chance.

    1. Puzzles. 2.   Mathematical recreations.   I. Title.
GV1493.M613   1986   793.7′4   86-40164
ISBN 0-394-74772-0

An Eddison · Sadd Edition
Edited, designed and produced by
Eddison/Sadd Editions Limited
2 Kendall Place, London W1H 3AH

Phototypeset by Bookworm Typesetting, Manchester, England
Origination by Columbia Offset, Singapore
Printed and bound in Hong Kong by Mandarin Offset
Marketing (H.K.) Ltd

The design on the front cover contains a visual puzzle.
What do these three-dimensional shapes carved from
cubes like blocks of stone represent?

CONTENTS

INTRODUCTION

I have always been fascinated by puzzles and games for the mind. I enjoy brain games of all types – and like particularly those with some special aspect or feature. Those I like best are not in fact always the hardest: sometimes a puzzle that is quite easy to solve has an elegance or a 'meaning' behind it that makes it especially satisfying. I have tried to provide a good selection in this book: some are easy and some are fiendishly difficult but they are all tremendous FUN! Above all, I have tried to provide something for everyone, in order to share my delight in such puzzles and games as widely as possible.

Solving puzzles is as much to do with the way you think about them as with natural ability or any impersonal measure of intelligence. Most people really should be able to solve nearly all the puzzles in this book, although of course some will seem easier than others. All it takes is a common-sense, practical approach, with a bit of logic and – occasionally – a little persistence or a flash of insight.

Thinking is what it's all about: comprehension is at least as important as visual perception or mathematical knowledge. After all, it is our different *ways* of thinking that set us apart as individuals and make each of us unique.

Although some of us feel we are better at solving problems mathematically, and others prefer to tackle problems involving similarities and dissimilarities, and others again simply proceed by trial-and-error persistence, we all have a very good chance of solving a broad selection of puzzles, as I'm sure you will find as you tackle those in this book.

From long and happy experience, however, I can tell you one secret, one golden rule: when you look at a puzzle, no matter how puzzling it seems, simply BELIEVE YOU CAN DO IT, and sure enough, you will!

HOW TO SOLVE PROBLEMS

To start things going, let's look at the different approaches that can be useful in solving puzzles.

First, the logical approach. Logic is always valuable, as it helps you work things out sequentially, using information received to progress step by step to the answer. In this book there are some puzzles in which logic is the perfect aid to finding the solution. As you might expect from its title, *Computer Patterns* is one of these.

In problem solving, there may also be a need for an 'indirect' approach, whereby you arrive at an answer by perceiving and thinking about a subject in a way you have never done before. This depends on how you think normally, of course, and so for some people it may be helpful for certain puzzles, and for others for different ones. The insight that leads you to an alternative way of solving the second part of *Count the Cubes* is a typical example.

The visual approach is also important, especially in this book because all the puzzles are presented in visual terms and require initial visual comprehension (or conceptualization) to be combined with understanding the text of the problem. This is an obvious requirement for puzzles of shape and form, most particularly where shapes must be searched for, as in *Hidden Shapes.*

In general, the puzzles in this book of games of *Shape* are of four types. They are concerned with:
1. distinguishing shapes (in 2 or 3 dimensions), especially where they have been broken up or dissected;
2. the orientation and reorientation of shapes;
3. comprehending changes in shape following specified transformations or changes in given circumstances;
4. visualizing and conceptualizing shapes or patterns from linear information (such as plans or maps).

Examples of all four types are given on the following pages, together with the answers. See if you can solve them first without looking at the answers – then go on to enjoy the rest of the book! If you have any queries about any of the puzzles, or you would just like to get in touch, please write to me care of the publishers. I shall be pleased to hear from you.

SAMPLE GAMES

GAME 1

Here is a mental jigsaw puzzle. Nine of the 12 numbered squares below make up the larger square and its pattern. Which squares fit where, and which three are redundant?

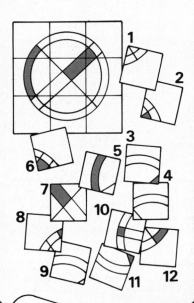

GAME 2

Two coins lie side by side. If the coin on the left is rolled around the coin on the right, in which direction will the head be facing when it reaches the other side? (This requires either a vivid imagination or a little mathematical knowledge.)

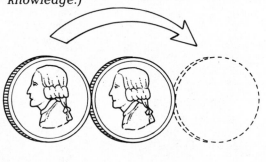

A. Although many people believe the coin would then be upside down, in fact it is right side up: the coin has traveled half way round the other – but has turned a full circle.

12	3	6	2
5	7	11	4
8	9	1	10

GAME 3

A coin is placed inside the bowl of a wine-glass shape made by four matches. Moving two matches – and only two – can you get the coin outside the glass?

You do not need to be familiar with wine-glasses to puzzle out the answer!

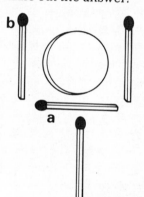

GAME 4

Imagine you are lying under a glass table looking up at six objects resting on the glass. You can see only their outlines, but you are told that you can see a ball, a square-bottomed vase with an oval lip, a hollow plastic pyramid, a watering can with a long spout that has a 'rose' attached, and two Christmas decorations – a bell and a star supported on its point. Can you work out which is which?

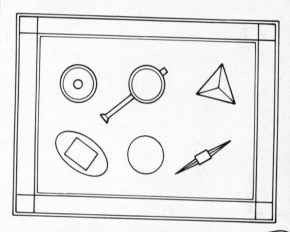

A Only the matches labeled a and b need be moved, to the positions shown.

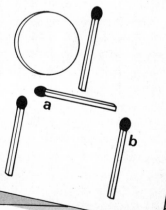

A

HIDDEN SHAPES

Shapes and patterns often disguise each other – this is part of the secret of camouflage. Here are six patterns and 12 shapes. All the patterns contain more than one shape. Can all the shapes be found? Can you find which shapes are hiding in which patterns?

Hint The shapes you are looking for in the patterns are exactly the same size as the ones outside. Also, three camouflaged shapes are partly concealed by the free shapes outside. Which are they?

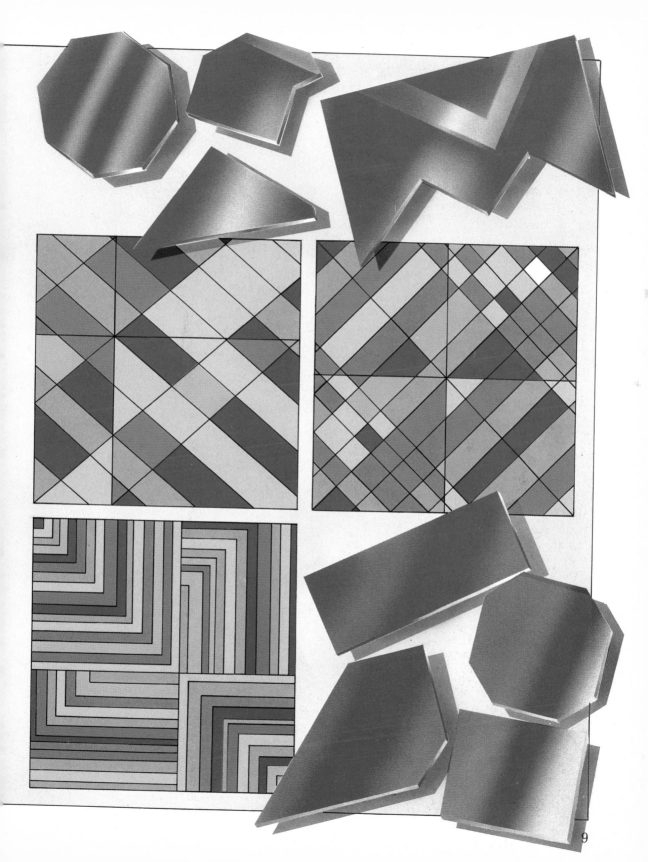

(Solutions page 51)

MATCH THE LINES

This puzzle contains a visual code created when the patterns of lines labeled 1 through 6 are combined with the patterns labeled A through G. To catch you out, I've deliberately made 11 combinations incorrectly. Which are they? Write your answers in the panel on the right.

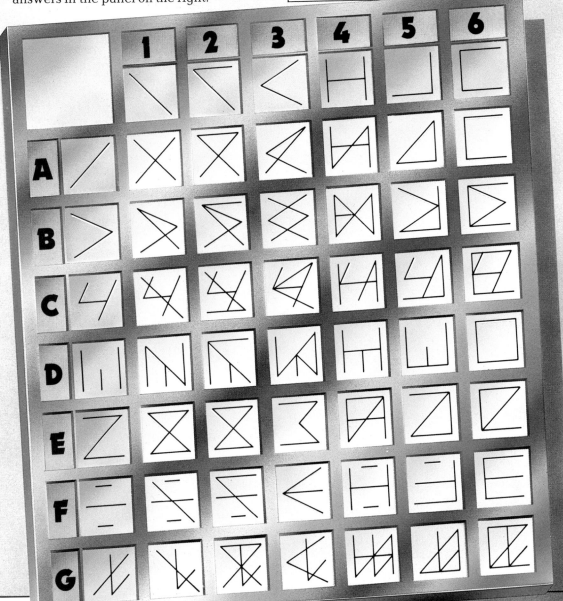

10

SQUARE THE MATCH

Everyone loves playing with matches . . . but not all match games are easy. These involve moving matches (or any movable short straight lines of the same length) to create new patterns made up of squares.

Moving only as many matches as directed, and creating as many squares as requested, can you complete these puzzles? (Squares may overlap or have corners in common.)

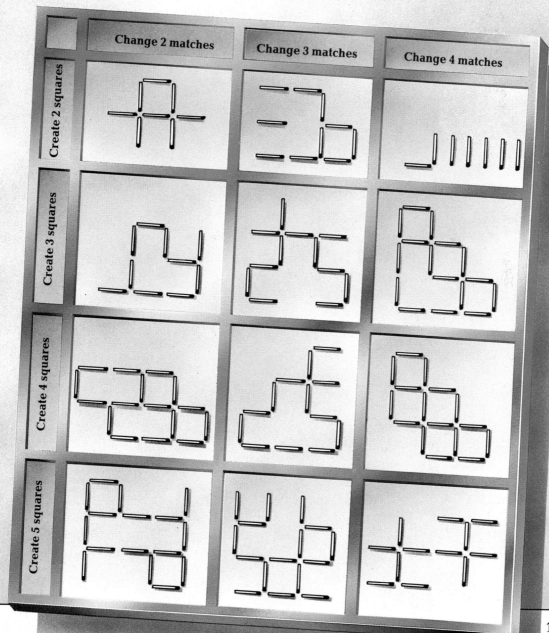

	Change 2 matches	Change 3 matches	Change 4 matches
Create 2 squares			
Create 3 squares			
Create 4 squares			
Create 5 squares			

(Solutions page 51, 52)

TRACKS AND TRACES

Michelangelo, the famous Italian painter and sculptor, is said to have been able to draw a perfect circle freehand. Don't panic – I'm not asking you to do that! But a circle is an excellent example of a continuous line that completes a pattern and returns to where it began. The puzzles below run along similar lines.

To draw the envelope-shaped design on the left (shape 1) with an unbroken line, start at the bottom left corner and follow the arrows. You can trace the pattern in one continuous line. Unlike a circle, however, this line does not end where it started.

Can you trace the other designs on these pages? In each one, put your pencil anywhere you wish to start, and see if you can complete the pattern without taking pencil from paper. In which ones can you make your line end where it started? Lines may cross but must not be retraced.

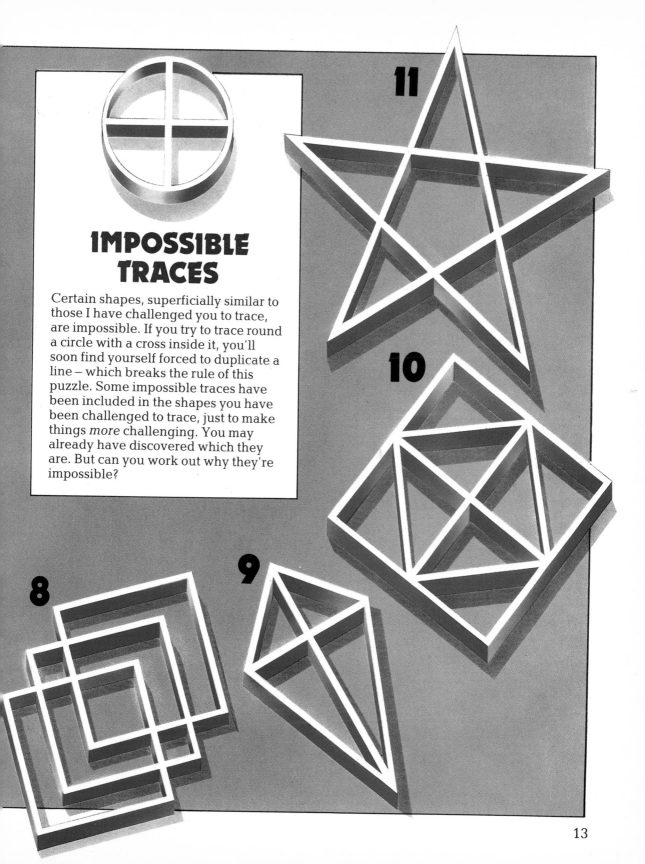

IMPOSSIBLE TRACES

Certain shapes, superficially similar to those I have challenged you to trace, are impossible. If you try to trace round a circle with a cross inside it, you'll soon find yourself forced to duplicate a line – which breaks the rule of this puzzle. Some impossible traces have been included in the shapes you have been challenged to trace, just to make things *more* challenging. You may already have discovered which they are. But can you work out why they're impossible?

11

10

8

9

(Solutions page 52)

COUNT THE CUBES

'Putting things into perspective' is a common phrase. Perspective not only helps to bring three-dimensional realism to a two-dimensional representation, it also helps us to interpret things we can't actually see, because it creates certain visual rules. In the designs below there are various combinations of cubes stacked together. Most are simple heaps – but some require you to understand that one or more rows of cubes go on behind others, out of sight. This is an example of a problem involving 'spatial relationships' which is the particular object of this puzzle.

GAME 1

Can you list the number of cubes in each stack, based on the visual evidence given, and with the further information that all rows of cubes are solid (complete) unless you can actually see them end?

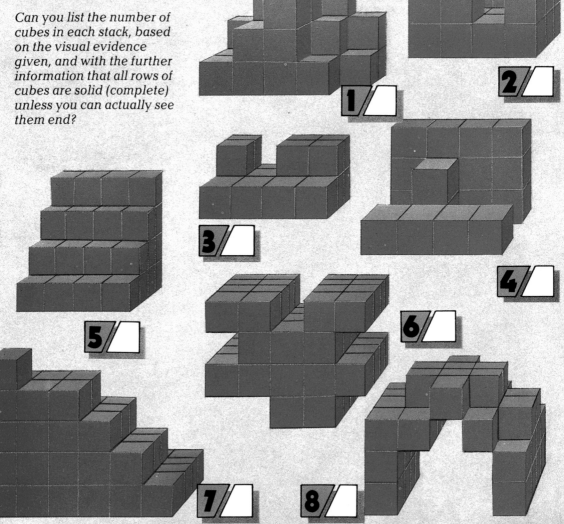

14

GAME 2

On this page the situation is reversed: parts of a large cube are missing — can you work out how many cubes in each case are not there? Having calculated a total number of missing cubes, notice that some (the outer ones) have dark colored surfaces: how many of the missing cubes would have been so colored on three sides, on two sides, on one side, or not at all? There is a score-box provided for your totals. There is a visual short-cut, too: can you work out what it is?

SCORE BOX

Missing cubes	1	2	3	4	5
Cubes colored on three sides					
Cubes colored on two sides					
Cubes colored on one side					
Not colored					
TOTALS					

(Solutions page 53)

DIVIDING THE SQUARE

Here's a popular type of puzzle that involves dividing a regular shape into different-shaped parts of equal area. To divide a square into halves of exactly the same shape (congruent) using an internal grid of two lines quartering the whole is relatively simple, and results in just three possible variants, as shown right.

Below and right are two series of squares with a 4 × 4 internal grid. In the first series, can you divide the squares into 6 different shapes, each being congruent halves, using the lines of the grid? In the second series, can you divide the series into 5 shapes comprising congruent quarters, using the lines of the grid?
Hint *Separate the shapes by thickening appropriate lines to create obvious boundaries to congruent parts, rather than shading in the shapes, as the latter can lead to confusion.*

Divide into quarters

Divide into halves

To solve the problem of quartering a square with a 6 × 6 internal grid is more difficult. Division can be based on two half-squares that are then halved again.

 Can you divide the squares below into quarters of the same area and shape using the lines of the internal grids?

One in each set of four has been done for you – can you do the other three? The problem is quite easy to solve once you have worked out the visual logic for grouping the squares into sets of four. **Hint** There are obvious equivalences in the ways that squares of a set of four are divided.

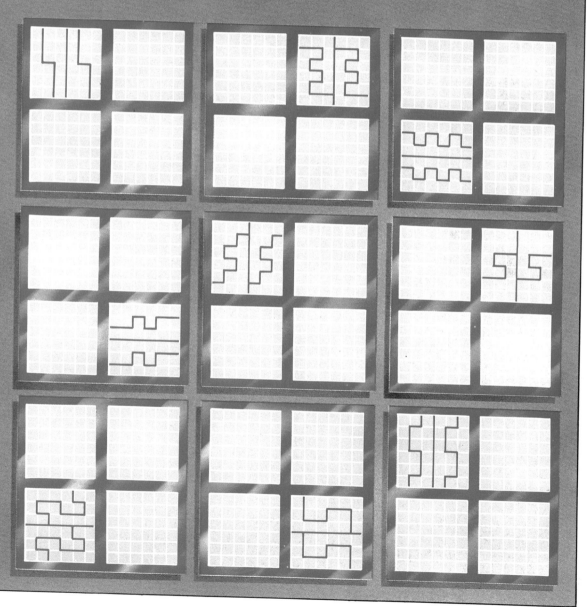

(Solutions page 54)

CUBE PROBLEMS

A cube placed with one side on a surface can be turned round to face any of four directions without being turned over. That's four directions per side, and the cube has six sides – so the total number of ways a cube can be placed on a surface is 6 × 4, or 24.

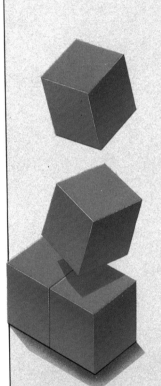

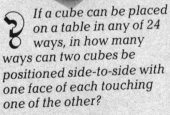

If a cube can be placed on a table in any of 24 ways, in how many ways can two cubes be positioned side-to-side with one face of each touching one of the other?

When three cubes are placed side by side, keeping in the same order, what is the total number of different ways the cubes can be turned, while keeping the same side-to-side arrangement?

Try again with eight cubes forming a greater cube. If the cubes remain in their present positions relative to each other but can turn every which way to touch those that are adjacent, what is the total number of ways individual cubes can be turned?

18

The six dice shown here represent different views of just a single dice; each view reveals three of its sides. Some symbols on the dice are missing however – and one of the views is deliberately misleading: it is from a completely different dice.

Can you work out what the missing symbols should be, based on the sides that are pictured? You may find it helpful to plot the overall plan of the completed dice, so an empty plan that can be filled in is provided below. Which is the different dice?

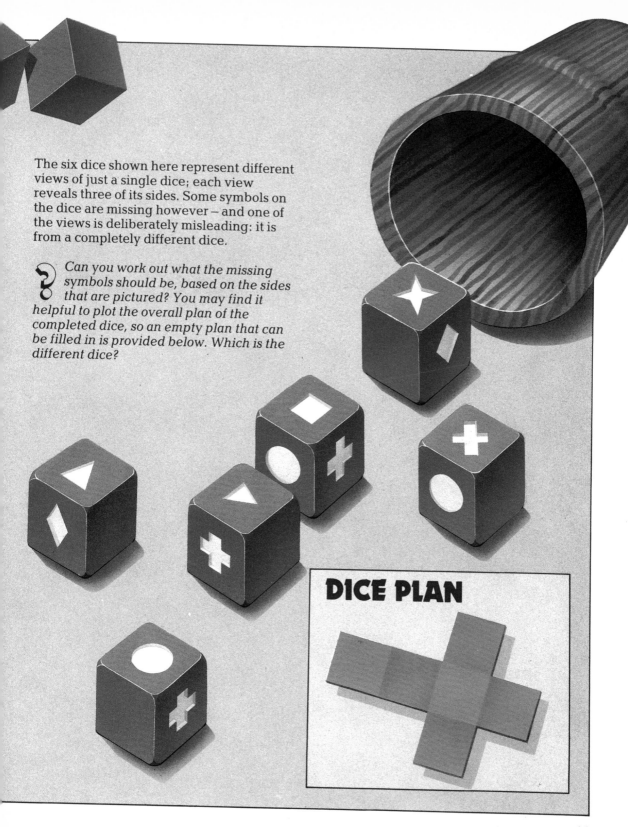

DICE PLAN

(Solutions page 54)

REPLI-TILES

Did you know that some shapes, if they are combined with a specific number of identical shapes of the same size, create a larger version of themselves? And, correspondingly, when such shapes are subdivided appropriately they also make smaller versions of themselves?

Well they do, and this is particularly evident with squares and equilateral triangles, as shown right. It is also true of many other regular three- and four-sided geometrical figures (of which the rhombus and the isosceles triangle are examples).

Among other shapes that can be subdivided into miniatures (or mirror-image miniatures) of themselves are rectangles from which one quarter has been removed. Shown below is a square which has had one quarter removed and then has been subdivided into four equal internal miniature versions of itself.

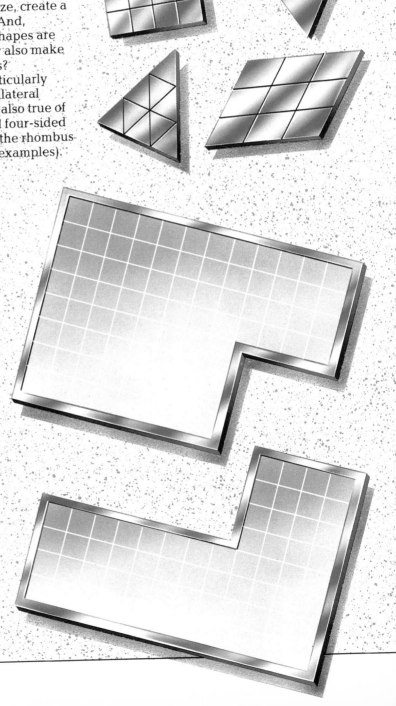

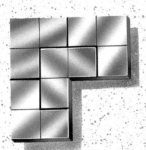

The same principles apply to the figures on the right. Can you subdivide them so that four miniatures can be created within each? A grid has been superimposed to help.

20

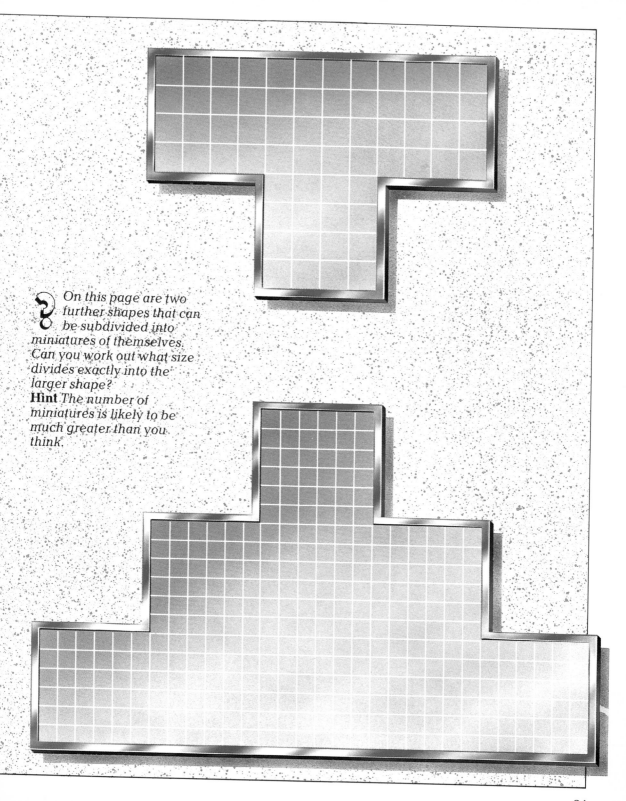

On this page are two further shapes that can be subdivided into miniatures of themselves. Can you work out what size divides exactly into the larger shape?
Hint The number of miniatures is likely to be much greater than you think.

(Solutions page 55)

REPLI-TILES 2

Here's another shape that can be subdivided into miniatures of itself – this time into small trapezoidal shapes, right, that (for the purposes of this puzzle, anyway) can be said to resemble a crab's shell. It's a shape that has no right-angles, unlike the repli-tiles on the previous two pages.

? On the beach fishing nets are laid out to dry. One is a hexagonal crab net (right). The crabs caught in it are the same as those the baskets contain. How many crabs will fit into the net? Can you find two different patterns for arranging the crabs in the net?

? Similar hexagonal nets (right) also catch fish. How many fishes of the shape shown can be caught in the net, if each fish retains its original shape?

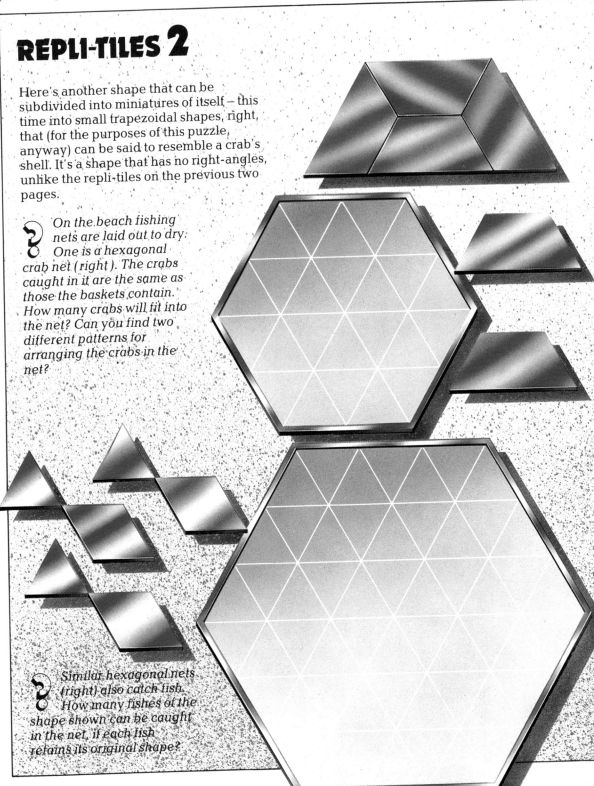

22

Large fishes also find these little ones delicious and, when they find a shoal, swallow as many as possible. If the small fishes remain whole, how many can fit into the large fish?

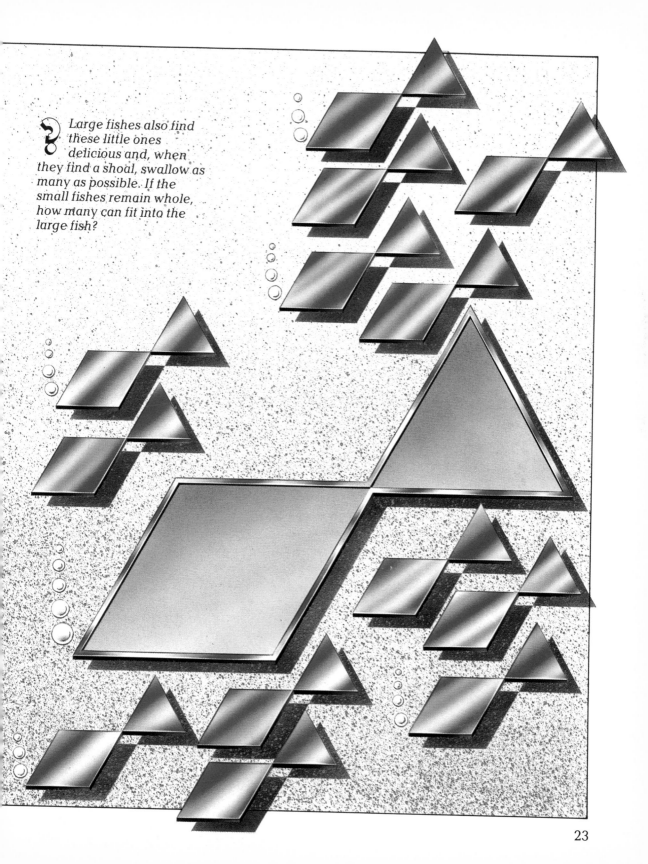

(Solutions page 55, 56)

ON THE REBOUND

The last pool ball is on the table: you have pocketed all the others and won the game easily. To celebrate, you plan to shoot that last ball from the bottom left-hand corner into a pocket to follow all the others – but you do not intend to shoot it directly. Your mastery of the game has to be demonstrated by pocketing the ball in as complex a way as possible, with at least two bounces off side cushions.

It is tricky to work out exactly where to aim the ball for its first bounce so that the identified pocket – the top left or the bottom right – is reached. It helps to imagine a grid superimposed over the table: the lines can be used as aiming markers at the edges of the table, and the squares can be used to judge that the angle at which the ball strikes a cushion is identical to that at which it rebounds.

GAME 1

You could use either of the courses shown right – but they are too easy, as they use only two side cushions. Can you work out, on the grids below, the path of a ball from the bottom left-hand corner a) to drop into the top left pocket, and b) to drop into the bottom right pocket, each time bouncing on at least three different side cushions?

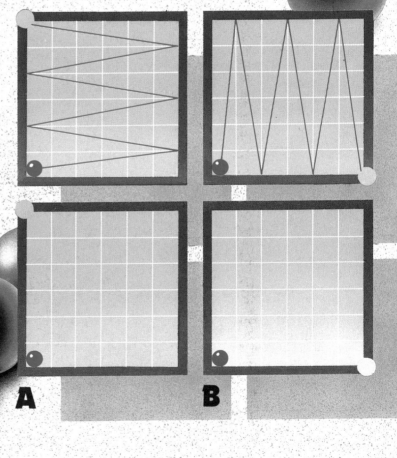

A

B

GAME 2

Even on an L-shaped table, to pocket the ball top left or bottom right has an easy way (shown on the two top tables) and a not-so-easy way. On the lower two grids, can you pocket the ball after bouncing it off at least four sides of the six, avoiding the central right-angle, with a) five bounces before going off at the top left and, for extra effect, b) seven bounces before going off at the bottom right?

Hint You may have to calculate proportions within the squares of the grid.

GAME 3

If you found those easy, try your luck with even more irregular tables (right). With the ball starting bottom left, can you work out paths for the ball to be pocketed a) top left, after three bounces each on a different side; b) top left of the right-hand section, after seven bounces; c) bottom right, after 13 bounces on five different sides? The ball may travel as long as is necessary. One of the three is in fact not possible. Which one?

Hint Avoid both central right-angles.

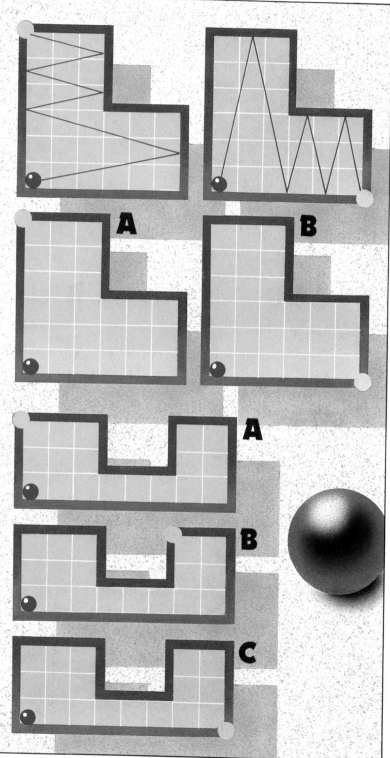

(Solutions page 56)

A PIECE OF CAKE

What could be easier than arranging the segments of these patterns so no two colored or numbered segments touch another of the same color or number? The more segments, the easier it is . . . or is it the other way around?

Either way, I'm sure you'll find this puzzle 'a piece of cake.'

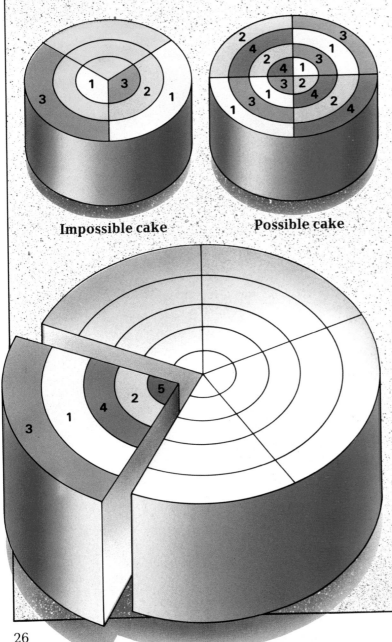

Impossible cake

Possible cake

The object is to color in the parts of the rings in the segments in such a way that the same color never touches itself, *even at a corner point.* I suggest you number the ring-sections first (in pencil which can be erased), and then use a color for each number. There should be as many colors as there are rings in the 'cake.'

For a three-segment, three-ring 'cake' the object simply can't be achieved with three colors. (So how many colors *are* required so that no one color touches itself even at a corner point, using as few as possible?)

The four-segment, four-ring 'cake' can be colored in according to the rules – but the final design is disappointingly symmetrical.

Is it necessarily so?

The five-segment, five-ring 'cake' follows the rules perfectly. Can you number and color it not only so that the five numbers (colors) never touch themselves even at a corner point, but also so that there is a complete range of numbers (colors) in each segment?

26

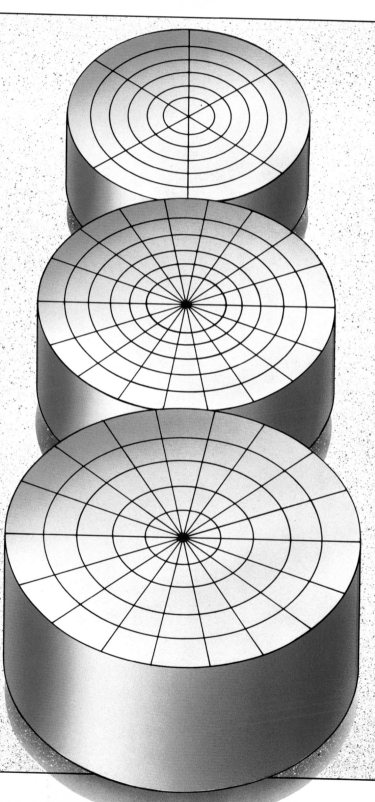

CAKE 1

The six-segment, six-ring 'cake' also follows the rules. Can you complete it as you did for the five-segment 'cake' opposite?

CAKE 2

Here is a variation on the theme: an 18-segment six-ring 'cake,' probably big enough for my next birthday! Can you number or color it using only six numbers or colors?

In case you make a mistake, it's a good idea to trace the design onto a separate sheet.

CAKE 3

Finally, here is an 18-segment five-ring cake. Can you do with it exactly what you were asked to do with the 18-segment six-ring cake above using five numbers or colors?

(Solutions page 57)

THE HOLLOW CUBE

Imagine you are peering into a hollow cube. At the bottom you can see a pattern of 6 × 6 squares. Another cube has a more regular pattern on an 8 × 8 grid. In both cases only bits of the pattern can be seen at any time. But there is enough information in what you can see for you to construct or deduce the patterns, bit by bit.

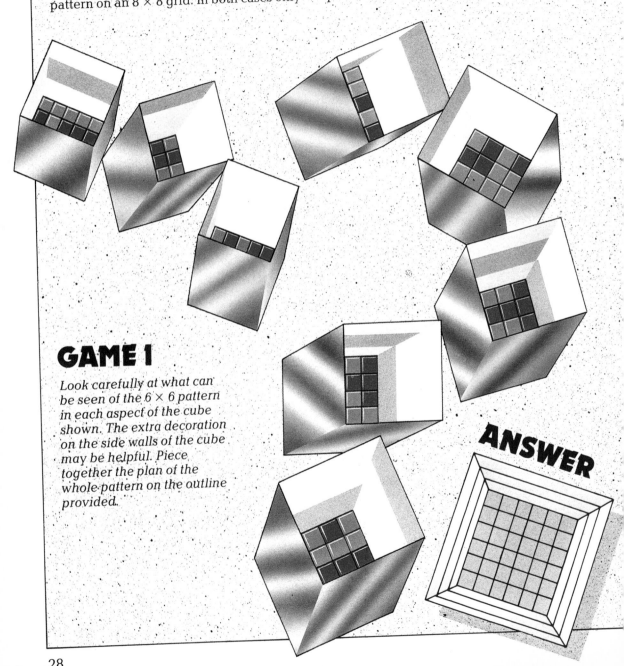

GAME 1

Look carefully at what can be seen of the 6 × 6 pattern in each aspect of the cube shown. The extra decoration on the side walls of the cube may be helpful. Piece together the plan of the whole pattern on the outline provided.

ANSWER

28

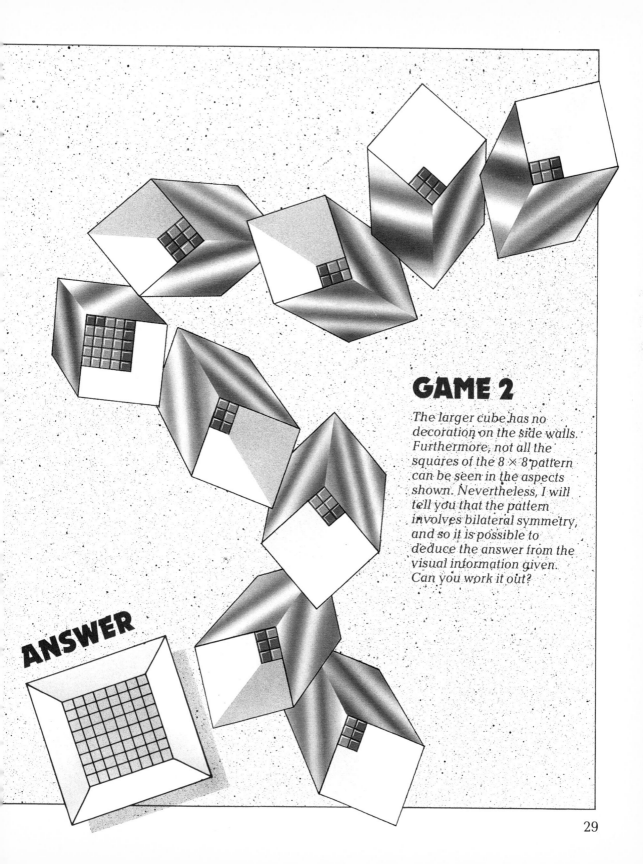

GAME 2

The larger cube has no decoration on the side walls. Furthermore, not all the squares of the 8 × 8 pattern can be seen in the aspects shown. Nevertheless, I will tell you that the pattern involves bilateral symmetry, and so it is possible to deduce the answer from the visual information given. Can you work it out?

ANSWER

(Solutions page 57)

HOW MANY?

Each of the designs on this page contains a number of figures of the same shape – squares, triangles or hexagons – in different sizes, some overlapping, some with common sides, some quite separate. Can you find them all?

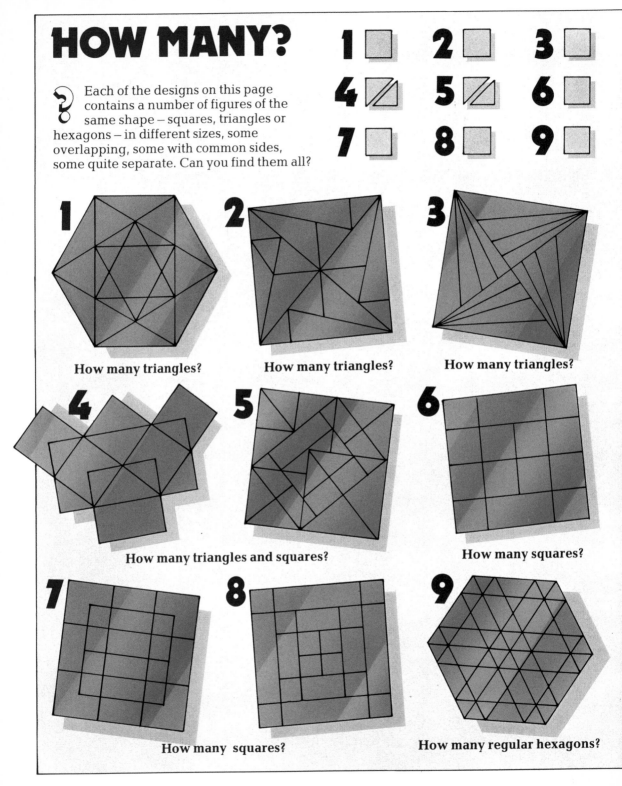

1 How many triangles?

2 How many triangles?

3 How many triangles?

4 How many triangles and squares?

5

6 How many squares?

7 How many squares?

8 How many squares?

9 How many regular hexagons?

PEGBOARDS

Pegboards are used in many games and educational activities. Almost all of them consist of squares divided into smaller squares: on this page I have represented the pegs or holes as dots, and the connectors between pegs as lines between dots. Some pegboards are arranged differently, but the same principles apply.

In a 4 × 4 pegboard, how many different sizes of square can you create by connecting pegs? How many squares can you find altogether?
Hint Squares do not have to have horizontal bases.

In the pegboard consisting of two crossed parallel rows of holes, how many squares – of any size – can you create by connecting pegs? As in the first puzzle, the squares do not have to have horizontal bases.

If this pegboard has a peg in every hole, can you remove six pegs so that every square you found before now has no more than three corners marked with pegs so that no squares of any size remain?

(Solutions page 58)

INSIDE-OUTSIDE

As you will know, the size of the inside of a shape depends on both the size *and* the shape of the outside. This can be demonstrated by taking a loop of cord and stretching it tightly between two points: a very thin strip is enclosed, with a small area. If the loop is made to form a circle, the area enclosed is considerably greater, although the perimeter – the length of the outside – has not changed.

If a pegboard has a band stretched around four pegs, enclosing an area (as shown below) can you calculate the area, in unit squares, enclosed, without measuring anything? The trick is to count the unit squares crossed by each length of band and calculate the proportion of area enclosed.

For each *part* square within the perimeter band there is an equivalent shape of exactly the same size somewhere outside the band: the result is that certain rectangles appear to be divided in half by the band, so the area of that rectangle on the *inner* side of the band is exactly half the total area of the rectangle. Use this principle to solve the problem. For practical purposes, assume the band is simply a line with no thickness.

The perimeters of all the figures below are identical in length. But how much area is enclosed (or covered) by each? And which has the largest area? Calculate the areas using the superimposed grid, in grid-square units, then fill in your answers.

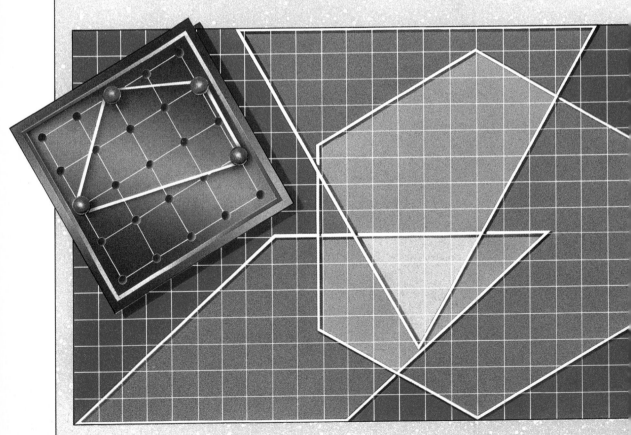

THE ISLAND PROBLEM

The ancient Greeks knew all about the significance of the perimeter in terms of the area enclosed – indeed, the word 'perimeter' derives from two Greek words meaning 'measure around.' Many of them lived on islands and had good reason to be aware of the pitfalls of area measurement. After all, it is easy to see that the area of an island cannot be assessed by the time it takes to walk around it: if the coastline is long, it does not necessarily mean that the island is large. Nevertheless the fifth-century writer Proclus tells us that some land-owners based real estate values on perimeter, not area.

An ancient story tells about Dido, legendary princess of Tyre, who fled to a certain spot in North Africa. Granted as much land there 'as could be covered by the hide of an ox,' she had the hide cut into thin strips and sewn together to make one long length. Then, using the shoreline as a natural boundary, she had her people stretch the hide cord out in as big a semicircle as possible, eventually enclosing an area of no less than 25 acres. It was this area that soon became the powerful and famous city of Carthage, scourge of the Romans.

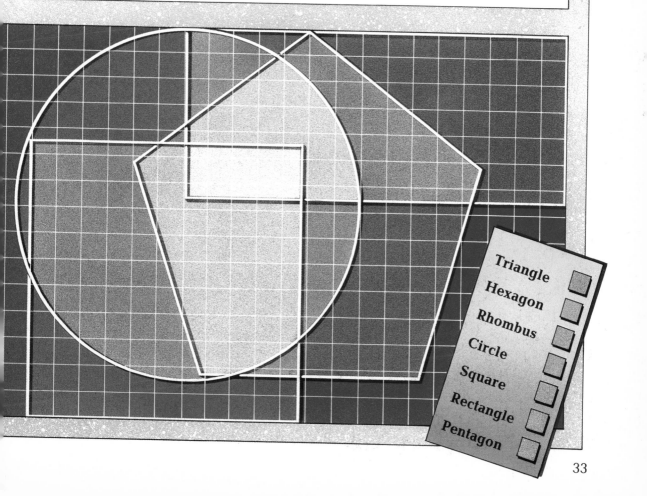

Triangle
Hexagon
Rhombus
Circle
Square
Rectangle
Pentagon

(Solutions page 58)

CUBES AND ROUTES

These strange robotic shapes floating in space and the oddly-made robot figure are designed to challenge your ability to think in three-dimensions.

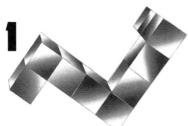

GAME 1

Isn't it surprising how different the same thing can look from a different angle? Believe it or not, in these 10 formations of cubes there are three identical pairs, one identical threesome – and one odd one out; it may take you some time, though, to see which is identical to which.

Hint *Rotating the book* may help.

When you have found the three pairs, the group of three and the odd one, write the appropriate numbers together in the answers box.

ANSWERS			
Three pairs			
Group of three			
Odd one out			

34

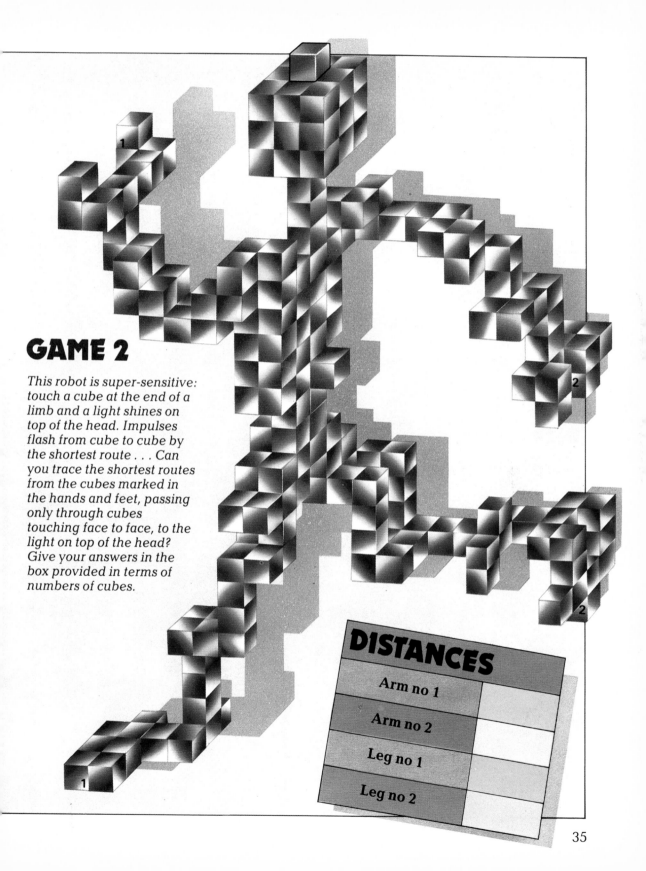

GAME 2

This robot is super-sensitive: touch a cube at the end of a limb and a light shines on top of the head. Impulses flash from cube to cube by the shortest route . . . Can you trace the shortest routes from the cubes marked in the hands and feet, passing only through cubes touching face to face, to the light on top of the head? Give your answers in the box provided in terms of numbers of cubes.

DISTANCES

Arm no 1	
Arm no 2	
Leg no 1	
Leg no 2	

(Solutions page 59)

FIND THE POLYGONS

At first glance the designs on these pages may seem no more than squares covered with crisscrossed lines, but look closer. Can you spot regularities and symmetries: squares, triangles, rhombuses, kite-shapes and so on? You certainly should be able to,

because this is the curious property of the design, which is remarkable for another reason, too. The whole pattern is actually made up of four equilateral triangles of the largest size possible within the square, with one point in each of the square's corners.

The puzzle is this: can you find all the different shapes listed, from 1 to 21? To make things easier I have provided one design for each set of shapes you are looking for. You can use pencils or pens of different colors to mark out each shape you find.

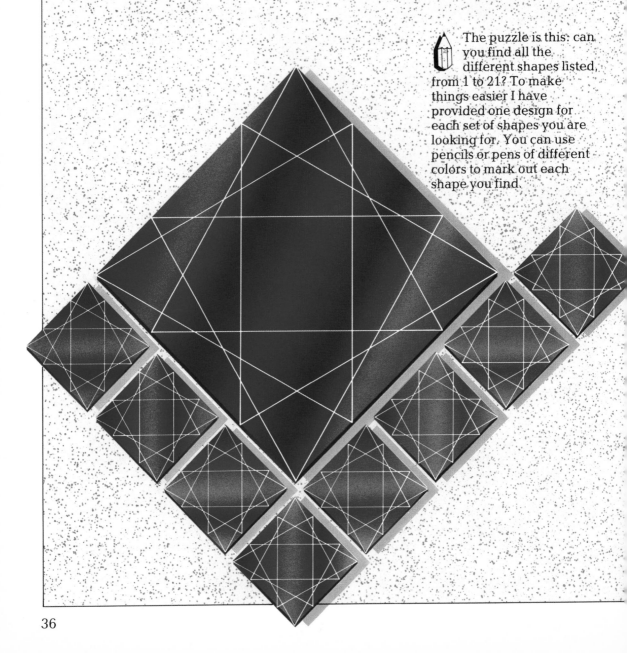

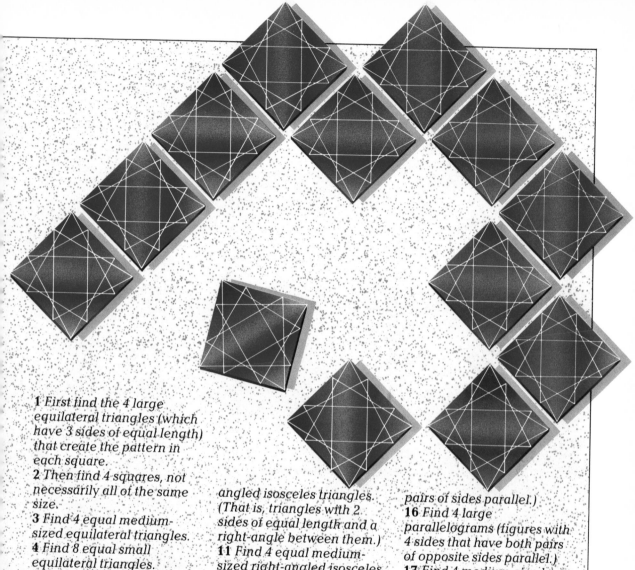

1 First find the 4 large equilateral triangles (which have 3 sides of equal length) that create the pattern in each square.

2 Then find 4 squares, not necessarily all of the same size.

3 Find 4 equal medium-sized equilateral triangles.

4 Find 8 equal small equilateral triangles.

5 Find 4 equal halves of a regular hexagon. (A regular hexagon is a shape with 6 sides of equal length.)

6 Find 2 equal large but irregular 6-sided shapes.

7 Find 2 equal medium-sized irregular 6-sided shapes.

8 Find 2 equal smaller irregular 6-sided shapes.

9 Find 1 irregular 8-sided shape.

10 Find 4 equal large right-angled isosceles triangles. (That is, triangles with 2 sides of equal length and a right-angle between them.)

11 Find 4 equal medium-sized right-angled isosceles triangles.

12 Find 8 large right-angled triangles that do not have sides of equal length.

13 Find 8 medium-sized right-angled triangles that do not have sides of equal length.

14 Find the 8 smallest right-angled triangles that do not have sides of equal length.

15 Find 2 equal large rhombuses (figures with 4 equal sides that have only 2 pairs of sides parallel.)

16 Find 4 large parallelograms (figures with 4 sides that have both pairs of opposite sides parallel.)

17 Find 4 medium-sized parallelograms.

18 Find 4 equal 5-sided shapes, that fit together to form the outline of the irregular 8-sided figure found previously (**9**.)

19 Find the 4 largest kite shapes (symmetrical about the longest axis.)

20 Find the 4 smallest four-sided kite-shapes.

21 How many different right-angled triangles can you find altogether?

(Solutions page 59)

MULTI-VIEWS

As your helicopter gently descends past a building to the ground, what do you see of the building? From high up you see only the roof laid out below you; then as you sweep down and to one side, there is a completely different view. Yet it is the same building. The puzzles on these pages involve combining such differing viewpoints.

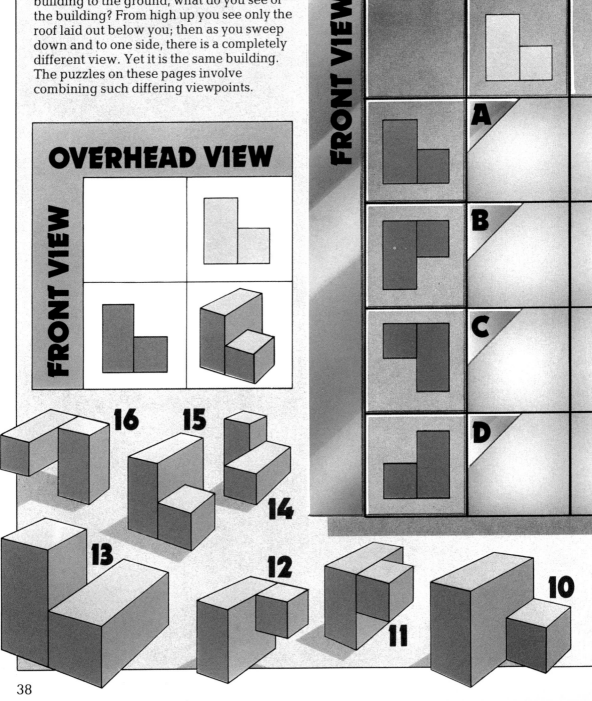

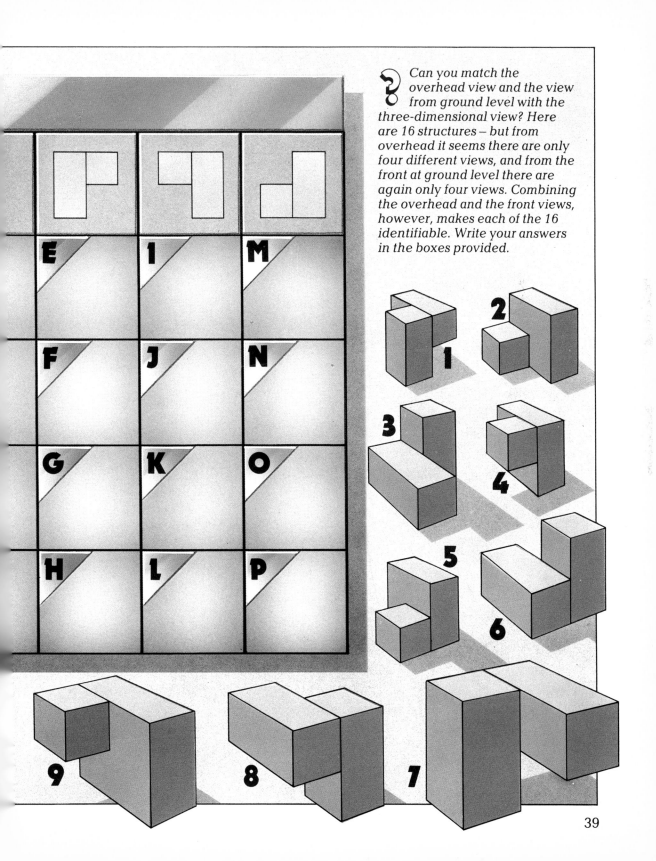

Can you match the overhead view and the view from ground level with the three-dimensional view? Here are 16 structures – but from overhead it seems there are only four different views, and from the front at ground level there are again only four views. Combining the overhead and the front views, however, makes each of the 16 identifiable. Write your answers in the boxes provided.

(Solutions page 60)

DISTORTRIX

Have you ever looked at yourself in the distorting mirrors you find at a fair? Their surfaces are curved instead of flat, so that parts of the image are enlarged, and other parts are made smaller.

If you imagine a face to be made up of small square patches, as if you are looking at it through a wire-mesh netting, a distorting mirror reduces some areas in comparison with others, enlarges some, and distorts many in different ways. On these and the next two pages are some distortions even stranger than those in fairground mirrors.

On the right is the basic design, which you should transfer, square by square, to the distorted grids on these two pages. Copy the part of the original outline in each original square onto the equivalent distorted 'square' in the distorted grid.

MASTER SHAPE

SHAPE 1

40

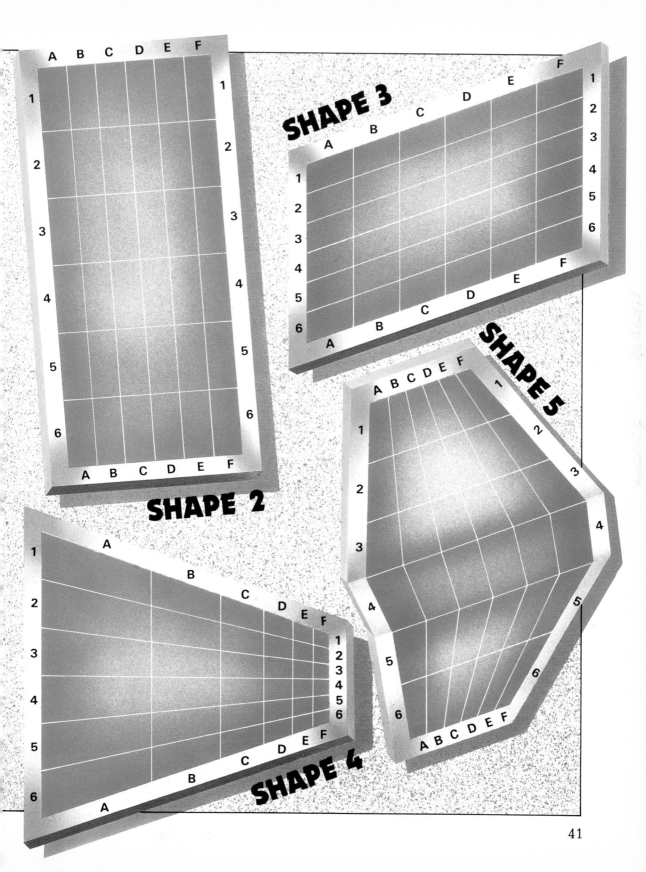

SHAPE 3

SHAPE 5

SHAPE 2

SHAPE 4

41

(Solutions page 60)

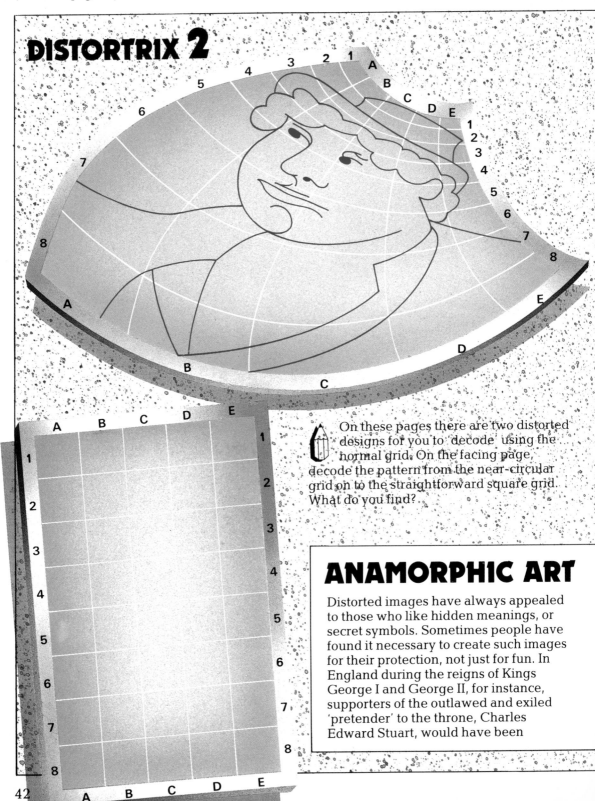

DISTORTRIX 2

On these pages there are two distorted designs for you to 'decode' using the normal grid. On the facing page, decode the pattern from the near-circular grid on to the straightforward square grid. What do you find?

ANAMORPHIC ART

Distorted images have always appealed to those who like hidden meanings, or secret symbols. Sometimes people have found it necessary to create such images for their protection, not just for fun. In England during the reigns of Kings George I and George II, for instance, supporters of the outlawed and exiled 'pretender' to the throne, Charles Edward Stuart, would have been

42

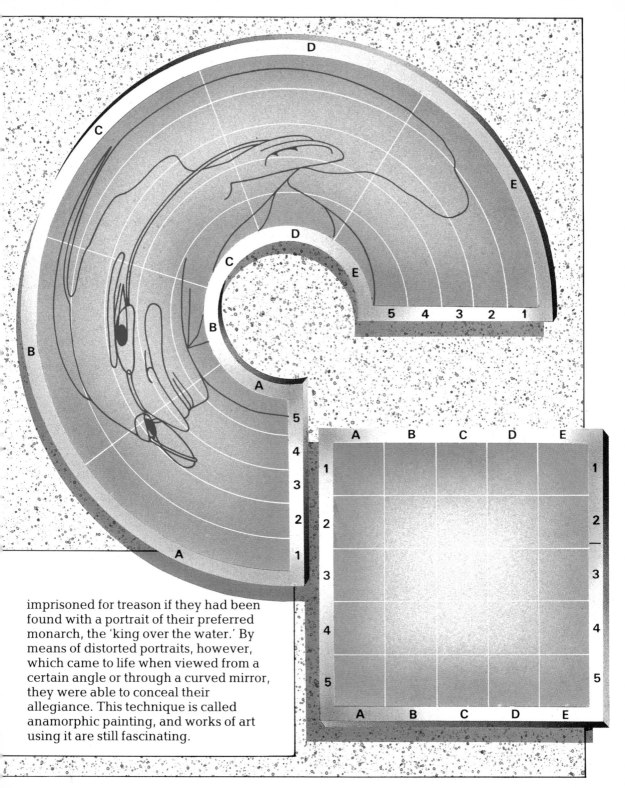

imprisoned for treason if they had been found with a portrait of their preferred monarch, the 'king over the water.' By means of distorted portraits, however, which came to life when viewed from a certain angle or through a curved mirror, they were able to conceal their allegiance. This technique is called anamorphic painting, and works of art using it are still fascinating.

SPACE FILLER

See if you can divide the large equilateral triangle on this page and the parallelogram on the opposite page into as few smaller equilateral triangles as possible, using the lines of the grid, so that all the space is filled. This is not quite so easy as it seems, as you will see from the explanation below.

Subdivision is quite easy when there are even numbers of grid-triangles on each side (as in **1** below). When there is an odd number of grid-triangles, however, things are rather different. After the first division, you will find there is space left over; following the rules, this also has to be divided into as few equilateral triangles as possible. In a triangle which has a number of grid-triangles per side divisible by 3, the method shown in **2** below is the most economic.

By a similar process, if the number of grid-triangles per side is divisible by 5, the method shown in **3** below is the most economic.

1

2

3

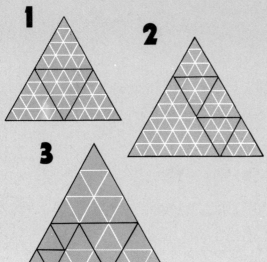

Following the rules, what is the least number of equilateral triangles into which you can divide this large triangle with 11 grid-triangles per side?

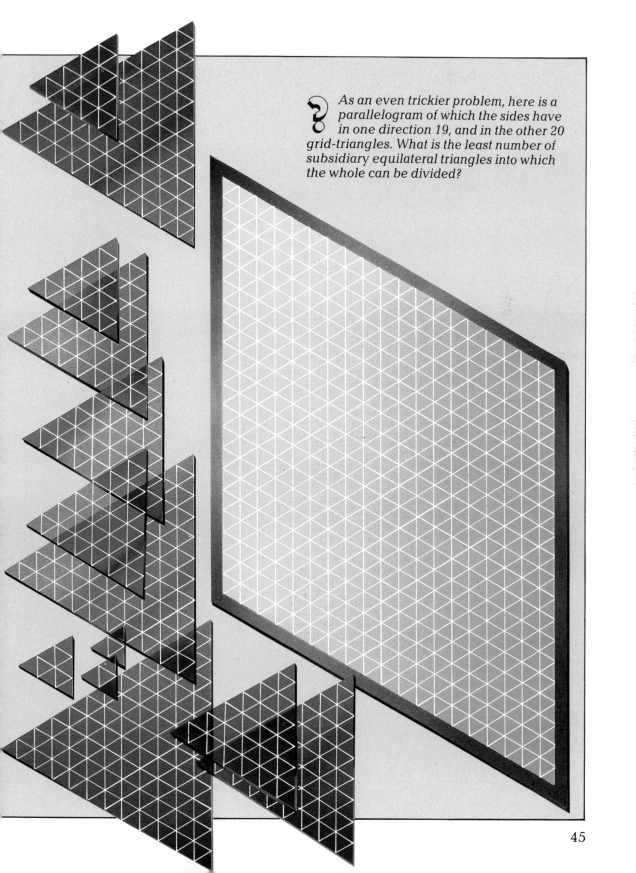

As an even trickier problem, here is a parallelogram of which the sides have in one direction 19, and in the other 20 grid-triangles. What is the least number of subsidiary equilateral triangles into which the whole can be divided?

45

(Solutions page 61, 62)

SUBWAYS

The subway is meant to be a quick way across town – and for many journeys it is. But in towns where there are more than two subway lines and just a few interconnecting stations, travelers have to get used to waiting around. And they have also to get used to time spent walking between platforms. On many subway systems, having to change trains is the equivalent in time of at least one more stop on the first train. And that is the statistic at the heart of the puzzles on these two pages.

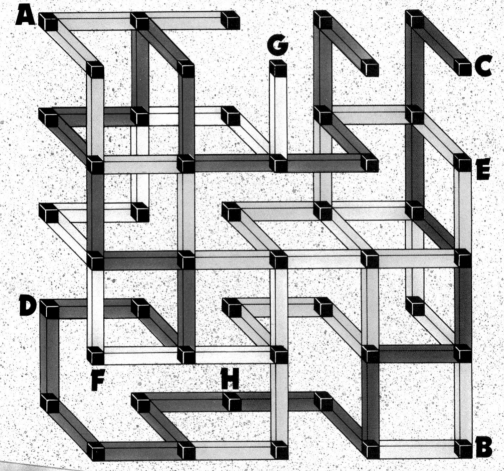

Find the shortest routes:

A to B ☐

E to F ☐

C to D ☐

G to H ☐

The object of this puzzle is to find the shortest route between specified stations (left), counting each station you pass (including the station you start at) as 1 unit of time (or, therefore, effective distance), and any station where you change lines as 2 units.

This puzzle is slightly more complex. Like the one on the previous page, however, this subway runs on two principal levels (representing a sort of three-dimensional cubic layout) – but this time there is another line between the two, connected only at certain stations. This is the express line: there are fewer stations and so trains travel faster. The snag is: there are fewer trains too. Also, the routes have been drawn at a more acute angle, so it is more difficult to be sure where you're going to end up!

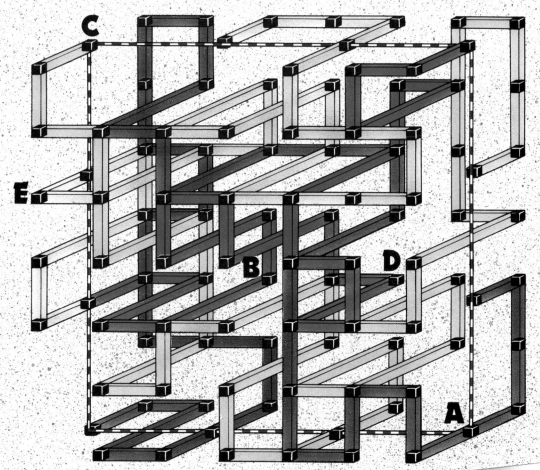

The object of this puzzle is to find the shortest route between specified stations (right), counting each station you pass (including the station you start at) as 1; any station where you change routes as 2, and each time you get on or get off the express line as 3.

Find the shortest routes:

A to B ☐   B to C ☐

C to D ☐   D to E ☐

47

COMPUTER PATTERNS

The universe we inhabit is vast and the laws of nature are complex. Even a simple self-contained system or 'universe', with simple laws, can still hold many surprises.

Modern computers operate like small universes: the programs that control what they do are their 'laws of nature.' Even a simple progressive program can produce a rich variety of results.

START

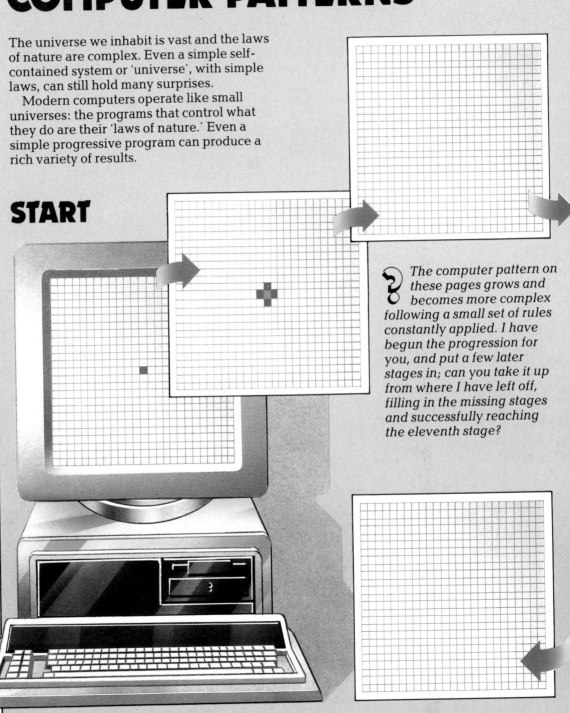

The computer pattern on these pages grows and becomes more complex following a small set of rules constantly applied. I have begun the progression for you, and put a few later stages in; can you take it up from where I have left off, filling in the missing stages and successfully reaching the eleventh stage?

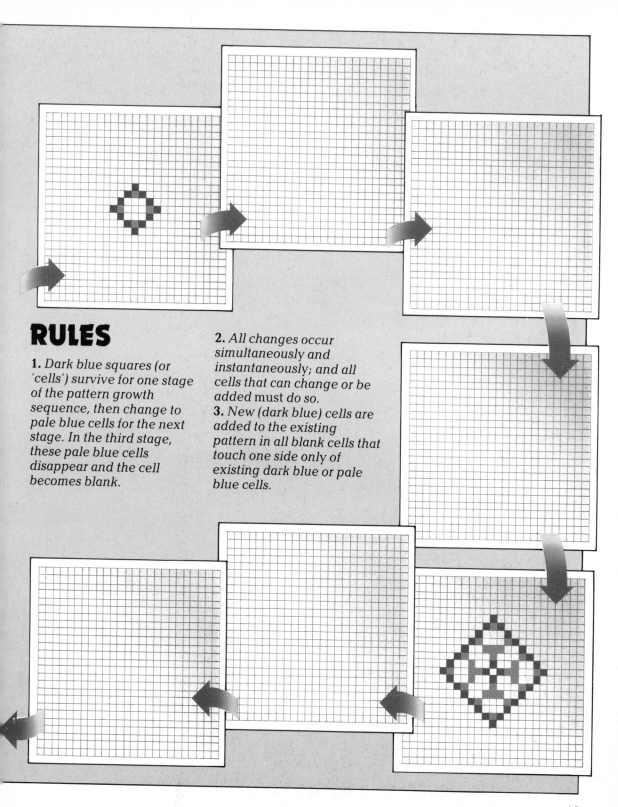

RULES

1. Dark blue squares (or 'cells') survive for one stage of the pattern growth sequence, then change to pale blue cells for the next stage. In the third stage, these pale blue cells disappear and the cell becomes blank.

2. All changes occur simultaneously and instantaneously; and all cells that can change or be added must do so.

3. New (dark blue) cells are added to the existing pattern in all blank cells that touch one side only of existing dark blue or pale blue cells.

THE SOLUTIONS

HIDDEN SHAPES PAGE 8-9

The five-sided kite shape, the large M-shape and one of the octagons are partly concealed by free shapes. That the hidden shapes can be identified easily nevertheless illustrates how our perception interprets what we see. A mechanical analysis would fail to recognize these partly concealed shapes because a small element of each is 'missing'.

One form of camouflage – perhaps observable in nature generally – is that which allows a gentle blurring of outlines, a simple fading into the background. Another, featured in these problems, is the deliberate creation of dominant patterns that distract the eye in a number of ways so that shapes within the patterns are rendered less obvious. Here we are confronted by a multitude of redundant lines which attract the attention by the geometrical regularity or angularity; by areas of color and shading which create their own forms; and finally by a number of shapes within the patterns that are misleadingly close – but not identical – to those being sought.

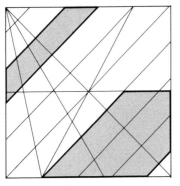

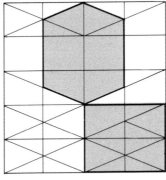

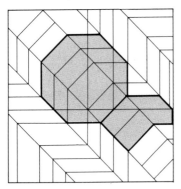

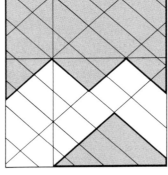

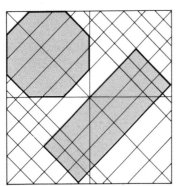

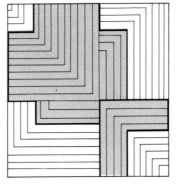

MATCH THE LINES PAGE 10

The deliberate errors are: A6 B4 C2 D2 D3 D6 E3 E4 F3 G1 G3

SQUARE THE MATCH PAGE 11

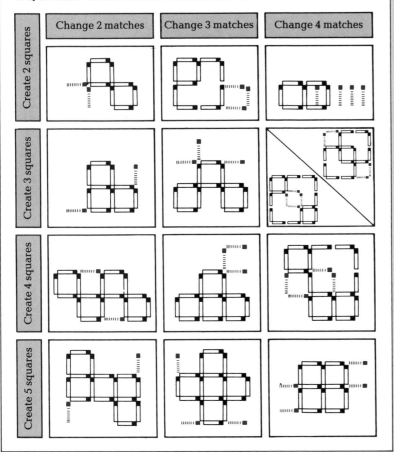

	Change 2 matches	Change 3 matches	Change 4 matches
Create 2 squares			
Create 3 squares			
Create 4 squares			
Create 5 squares			

SQUARE THE MATCH

As with many match problems, the trick with these is to visualize the correct final form before moving any matches at all. Some, for example, end up in squares of different sizes; some overlap; and many have common sides. But this is not to say that the trial-and-error approach cannot succeed: for most people confronted by problems like this it is the only way. Moreover, by actually moving the matches – or drawing the moves on paper – it is possible to work toward the solutions to these puzzles, to progressively come to an understanding of what size of squares you are looking for and see if any should overlap. With this experience it is entirely possible for most people to go on to devise their own more complex puzzles to set their friends.

TRACKS AND TRACES

A famous problem also based on the possibility or impossibility of a single continuous line connecting a complex circuit concerns the seven bridges in and around the town of Königsberg. The townspeople were said for centuries never to have been able to solve the question: could they go for a stroll, crossing each bridge only once, and end up where they began?

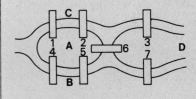

Konigsberg Bridges

TRACKS AND TRACES PAGE 12-13

Shapes 2, 3, 4, 5, 6, 7, 8, and 11 are possible to trace around without taking pencil from paper, as shown below.

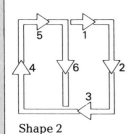

Shape 2

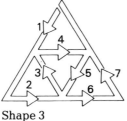

Shape 3

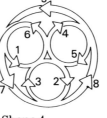

Shape 4

TRACKS AND TRACES contd

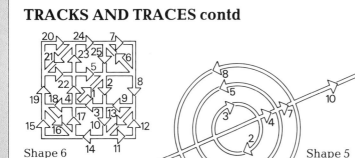

Shape 6

Shape 5

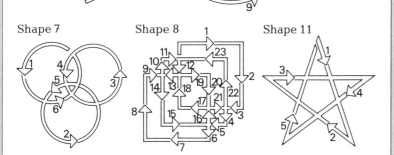

Shape 7   Shape 8   Shape 11

IMPOSSIBLE TRACES

Shapes 9 and 10 cannot be successfully traced. They are both versions of the 'impossible' shape shown on page 13.

The general rule is that if there are more than two junctions with an odd number of tracks, the route cannot be traced. If there are two odd-number junctions, the design can be regarded as borderline: if it can be traced, the line will not end at the starting point. Choosing the right starting point is an important key to discovering the trace.

The eminent eighteenth-century Swiss mathematician Leonhard Euler eventually proved that it could not be done. To do so, he constructed thematic drawings posing the same problem geometrically. Below, drawn in this way, are two modern versions of the same problem which are said thus to have 'topographical equivalence' to the original. In all of them, from the original physical problem onward, if you were allowed just one break in the sequence – if having crossed the third bridge you could start from somewhere else toward the fourth – you would be able to cross all seven points and find yourself where you started.

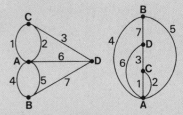

topological equivalent

COUNT THE CUBES PAGE 14-15

Game 1
1 – 30 cubes   **2** – 20 cubes
3 – 18 cubes   **4** – 18 cubes
5 – 40 cubes   **6** – 56 cubes
7 – 58 cubes   **8** – 38 cubes

Game 2
Your score box should look like the chart on the right. The visual clue suggested on page 15 is to turn the page upside down, which makes the 'missing' cubes appear solid.

MISSING CUBES	1	2	3	4	5
Colored on three sides	1	1	1	1	1
Colored on two sides	6	6	6	3	10
Colored on one side	12	12	12	3	19
Not colored	7	—	1	—	6
TOTALS	26	19	20	7	36

DIVIDING THE SQUARE

The final game shows only 36 ways of dividing a 6 × 6 square into four congruent parts. There are in all more than 96 possibilities, all in four variants of each theme (in rotations and mirror-images); there is also inevitably one final method of division, the simplest possible – into four squares of 3 × 3 each. This has to remain an individual variant, because it looks the same whether rotated or as mirror-image.

You may like to continue, by careful analysis and progression, to work out all the other variants.

COUNT THE CUBES

These problems depend on our perception of depth, the three-dimensional effect afforded by perspective, in two dimensions. So well is this effect now understood – although either unknown or ignored for millennia before medieval times – that computers can be programmed to recognize three-dimensional objects (such as a particular programmer's facial features in any expression) at any angle, and holograms are not merely works of art to marvel at but used for commercial and security purposes. Yet it is also well known that perspective can be misleading. Most of us at one time or another have seen the carefully-constructed room scenario in which a person who crosses the floor from left to right appears to shrink – in which, in fact, the room is not square at all and by walking from left to right the person is really walking steadily away from the viewpoint.

No such tricks are included in these puzzles. All the same, as I implied in my second question, there is a visual short-cut to the answer that is a direct result of the vagaries of perspective. Hold the book upside down: most people will now see the 'missing' cubes as the only solid cubes – which are naturally much easier to count; the painted cubes now appear as a sort of tiled surround.

DIVIDING THE SQUARE PAGE 16-17

If you shaded in the halves and quarters, there is always the danger that you would count one variant *and its opposite* as separate ways of dividing the square.

The five ways of dividing a 4 × 4 grid square in quarters are:

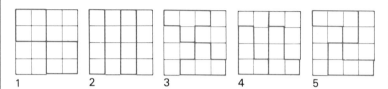

1   2   3   4   5

The six ways of dividing a 4 × 4 grid square in half are:

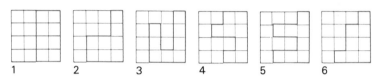

1   2   3   4   5   6

The completed sets of 6 × 6 grid squares divided into congruent quarters are shown below:

The visual logic has two elements: the pair of upper squares and lower squares are mirror images; the lower squares are simply 90° rotations of the upper ones.

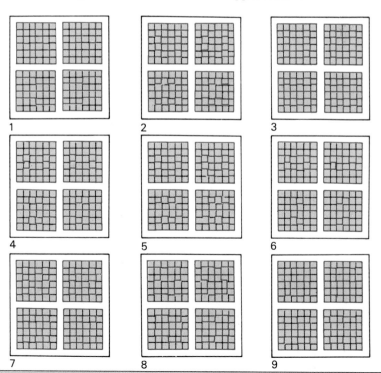

1   2   3
4   5   6
7   8   9

CUBE PROBLEMS PAGE 18-19

Q1. Keeping one cube still, while the other turns, allows 24 variations. Rotating both cubes, the variations possible total $24 \times 24 = 576$.

Q2. Similarly – and as long as the cubes remain in the same order – the variations possible with three cubes therefore total $24 \times 24 \times 24 = 13,824$.

Q3. As long as the cubes within the formation of eight keep to the same positional arrangement – and counting a single turn of one face of one cube as a variation of the whole pattern – then the number of ways the whole pattern can be changed is 24 times itself 8 times or 110,075,314,176.

GAME 2
This is what the dice should have looked like with the missing symbols filled in:

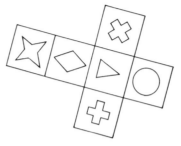

The different dice, sneakily, was the one not to feature a blank space. But its symbols as shown simply will not fit with the other views of the subject dice.

CUBE PROBLEMS

Game 1 (Q2, Q3)
Changing the order of the three cubes and the eight cubes multiplies the factorial figure by the number of variations then possible in each case.

For example, with three cubes there are three possible different arrangements of the cubes (ABC, BAC and ACB – the other three possibilities merely reverse each of these and are not statistically important, therefore). And for each of these orders there are 13,824 variations. So the actual total possible in these circumstances is $3 \times 13,824 = 41,472$.

You may like to go on to work out in exactly the same fashion the total number of variations possible with the eight cubes, given that there are 20,160 different positional arrangements of eight cubes in this formation. The answer is something greater than 2.219×10^{15}.

Game 2
This puzzle is made particularly difficult because the 'normal' situation, in which three sides of each cube would allow the others to be deduced straightforwardly, is confused by the faces deliberately left blank. The false trail of the extraneous dice adds to the confusion. The problem can only be solved by forming known pairs of sides and building up the complete picture from these.

REPLI-TILES 1 PAGE 20-21

The T-polygon contains 16 miniatures, and the stepped polygon contains 36. The two L-shaped figures each contain four miniatures.

REPLI-TILES 2 PAGE 22-23

Q1. There are eight crabs caught up in the net. See the two different patterns below:

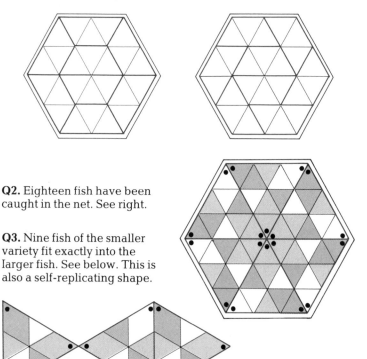

Q2. Eighteen fish have been caught in the net. See right.

Q3. Nine fish of the smaller variety fit exactly into the larger fish. See below. This is also a self-replicating shape.

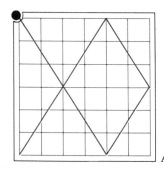

REPLI-TILES (1) AND (2)

Most of us have seen a kitchen floor covered in tiles in checkerboard pattern, alternating black and white squares in a severe but not unpleasing geometrical pattern. Many of us, I suppose, have also seen similarly regular pieces of mosaic or parquet work. The design is not always formed of squares, of course: diamonds, triangles, rhombuses and hexagons are also suitable for covering an area decoratively. And the art of doing so is called tessellation.

Except for four-sided patterns, however, it is rare for such tessellations to cover a regular area exactly; usually there are some half- or quarter-patterns left over round the edges. It is rarer still for tesseral patterns to combine to make larger versions of themselves, as the ones shown in these puzzles do.

Tessellation tends to be rare in nature, too. Probably the only field in which it occurs relatively often is crystallography.

ON THE REBOUND PAGE 24-25

The paths of the rebounding balls are shown on this page and the next. The impossible shot is on table B of Game 3.

Game 1

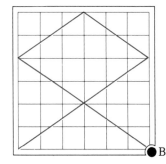

A

B

ON THE REBOUND

The impossible shot is table B of Game 3. After seven bounces the ball nearly reaches the pocket – but not quite. Accurate calculation proves this – but, if you drew the line freehand, the temptation to make the ball reach the pocket would almost certainly have been too great and you would have persuaded yourself it was possible after all.

For these games I have carefully stated that the ball may travel for as long as is necessary to reach the pocket. But in a real pool game, of course, other factors intrude and have to be considered as additional hazards by each player. Having been set in motion, a ball decelerates and eventually comes

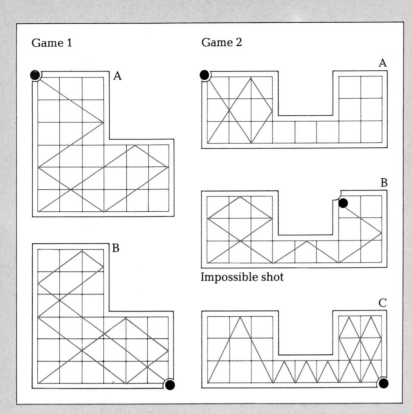

Game 1

Game 2

A

A

B

Impossible shot

B

C

to a standstill (unless it drops into a pocket first) through the effects both of friction against the cloth surface and of the loss of momentum caused by rebounding off a cushion.

It is possible to introduce the idea of such an 'entropy' factor into these games by speculating how many of the puzzles remain capable of successful completion if, for instance, the initial speed of the ball is reduced by a proportion (say 2 per cent) for every grid square wholly or partly crossed (giving a maximum total of squares crossed of 50, therefore), and by a greater proportion (say 10 per cent) for every bounce . (You may choose whatever percentage proportions you think suitable, naturally.)

Further mathematical considerations may also be introduced at your discretion to represent such effects as spin or stun.

A PIECE OF CAKE
PAGE 26-27

Because many rings of the segments in a three-segment cake interconnect with several others, no fewer than seven numbers or colors are required. The design of the coloration of the four-segment cake is inevitable, following the rules. The other cakes are drawn and numbered for you as shown here.

Cake 1

Cake 2

Cake 3

THE HOLLOW CUBE PAGE 28-29

The correct patterns are revealed below. Did you manage to deduce the 8 x 8 stylized capital M?

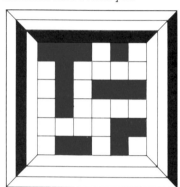

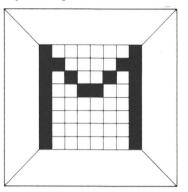

HOW MANY? PAGE 30

Each game is represented with its answer in the boxes alongside.

1 69   2 36   3 52

4 13/10   5 36/7   6 18

7 25   8 31   9 15

PEGBOARDS PAGE 31

Q1. There are 20 squares made up of five different sizes, as shown.

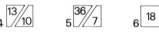

Q2. You can create 17 squares. If you count all squares formed when pegs are joined, even though they may not have pegs in each corner, the answer is 31.

Q3. The six pegs to remove are:

THE HOLLOW CUBE

These puzzles depend just as much on logic as they do on observation. Logic is required to sort out the evidence and make enough sense of it to be able to fill in as much of the answer panel as there is information. But in the second puzzle, the information is not all there, and again logic is required in order to deduce a symmetrical solution. I'm emphasizing the need for logic here because it is often the case that particularly observant or particularly logical people are perplexed (or at least inhibited) if there is an element of the puzzle that is unknown and therefore requires deduction (or intuitive guessing) to be used at the same time as more 'mechanical' logic.

HOW MANY?/PEGBOARDS

For many people the most difficult part of these problems will be keeping count. The first game in particular requires the ability to categorize sufficiently to be able to separate all the forms in each pattern that are of a certain size, before proceeding to count all those in the same pattern of the next size. Probably, some people are considerably better at this – possibly through experience – than others.

Variations in scale are also problematical in the second and third games, particularly in relation to squares which do not have a horizontal base.

INSIDE-OUTSIDE PAGE 32-33

The answers for the total area of the figures can be checked by simple mathematics. The formula for the area of a square, rectangle or rhombus is length of base × vertical height, and for a circle it is pi (π = 3.142) × radius squared. The pentagon and octagon can be divided into triangles, of which the areas can be calculated, then multiplied by 5 or 6 respectively.

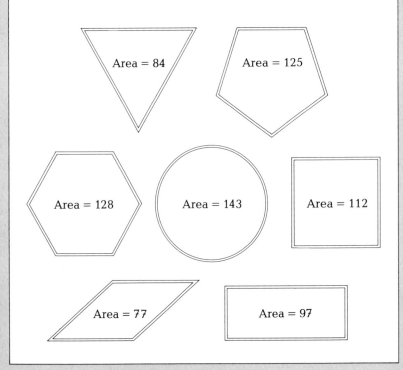

Area = 84

Area = 125

Area = 128

Area = 143

Area = 112

Area = 77

Area = 97

CUBES AND ROUTES PAGE 34-35

The solutions to the three-dimensional cubes are listed below.

Game 1

ANSWERS			
3 Pairs	1,8	4,10	7,5
Group of 3			2,3,9
Odd one		6	

Game 2

DISTANCES	
Arm No 1	27
Arm No 2	28
Leg No 1	37
Leg No 2	37

CUBES AND ROUTES

The very fact that the same thing can look totally different from a different viewpoint – so that our perception of it is altered although our awareness that it remains the same is constant – is often exploited by realist painters, particularly painters of outdoor and natural scenes. Many, before declaring a painting finished, survey the subject again through a mirror or, turning their back on the subject and bending over, even through their own legs, thus obtaining a different view of the subject they have just painted – a mirror-image version or one that is upside-down. By doing so, they get a new idea of salient features of the subject that they may then wish to add to the work.

Such aspects of perception go to prove that the conscious mind works in three-dimensional images, stored and related for use in categorizing and memorizing everything we see, and generally available to recall in such a way as to make comparison and recognition possible even from unfamiliar angles. In fact, we are ordinarily making use of this faculty for comparison and recognition every moment of our waking experience – and, if someone loses it (as occasionally happens through brain damage following accident or disease), everyday life becomes devastatingly complicated.

Game 2
The robot can also be treated as a game for two players: one races from Hand 1 to Foot 1, the other from Hand 2 to Foot 2 – but no cube can be occupied by more than one player, and a cube once used is 'out of bounds' to both players until the end of the game. Some fairly vicious tactics of blocking and evasion are possible . . .

FIND THE POLYGONS PAGE 36-37

As you can see below, the number of possible shapes that can be found within this simply constructed pattern are almost limitless.

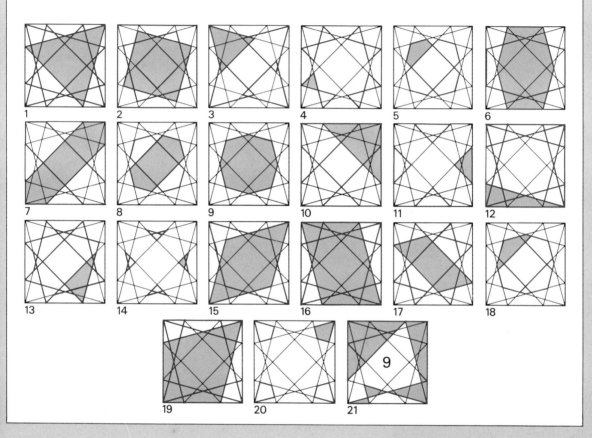

MULTI-VIEWS PAGE 38-39

The 16 views are combined correctly in the table below.

A	15	E	10	I	14	M	13
B	11	F	12	J	7	N	1
C	8	G	16	K	9	O	4
D	6	H	3	L	2	P	5

MULTI-VIEWS

These problems combine spatial awareness with logic – the ability to visualize in three dimensions from two-dimensional views.

In fact, the overhead views and front views given correspond fairly well to what architects call a plan and a front elevation. The plan represents the shape as laid out horizontally on the ground – the elevation is a front view that is derived exactly and immediately from the dimensions of the plan. Other elevations derived by architects in the same way are those of the remaining sides of the building, each seen as a direct face-on view, with no perspective.

DISTORTRIX 1 PAGE 40-41

The distorted image is reproduced for all the shapes, below.

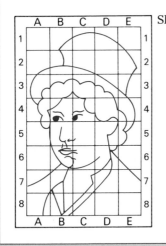

Shape 2

Shape 3

Shape 4

Shape 5

DISTORTRIX (1) and (2)

Toward the end of the nineteenth century there was considerable debate, in the light of the revelations made by Charles Darwin, over whether evolution in fact also worked on the principles of distortion from one original 'plan' of a creature to its next evolved stage. Much of the discussion was spurious but the fact remains that evolution has in many cases extended in a way that does indeed correspond closely to a distorted framework. (On the other hand, there are even more cases in nature where two creatures that bear some resemblance in form – different sizes, perhaps, or one a longer, thinner version of the other – are not in reality closely related by evolution.)

It may interest you to create further distortions that can be resolved by using a cylindrical mirror (which it is not too difficult to make from a length of shiny foil wrapped around a household cardboard tube). The curved shape required is that of Shape 3 (which can of course itself be utilized for this purpose in conjunction with a reflecting cylinder of the same diameter as the central near-circle).

DISTORTRIX 2 PAGE 42-43

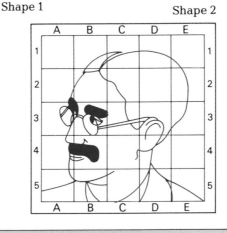

Shape 1

Shape 2

SPACE FILLER PAGE 44-45

Q1. The least number of equilateral triangles into which the large triangle can be divided using the triangles of the grid is 11. The triangles above the grid were a sort of hint.

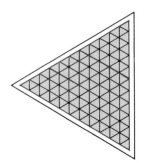

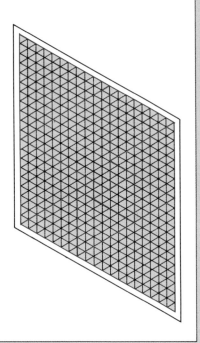

Q2. The least number of equilateral triangles into which the 19 × 20 grid parallelogram can be divided is 13. Did you notice that the triangles to the left and below the grid were a sort of hint?

SPACE FILLER

These puzzles again reflect the principles of tessellation (see Repli-tiles, pages 20-23) – covering a regular area with a regular pattern that may or may not be related in shape. But here it is not the tessellation that is important so much as the concept of filling the area using the lines of that tessellation (which may be helpful or unhelpful) as a guide.

SUBWAYS PAGE 46-47

Line diagrams of the subways show the shortest routes for each problem.

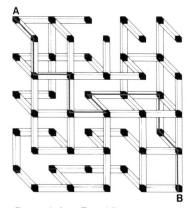

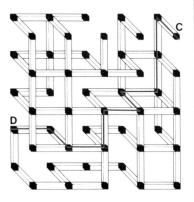

Game 1 A to B = 13

C to D = 13

SUBWAYS

More complex versions of both these games can be played by imagining that one or another line is out of service.

Both can also be played competitively by two or more players, who start at points apparently equidistant from an agreed destination. The race begins, taking alternate moves, station by station and where appropriate remaining for two or three turns (when changing lines). No station can be occupied by more than one player; when blocked in this way, a player must nevertheless make a move, even if it has to be backward.

You may devise your own subway line systems following similar principles.

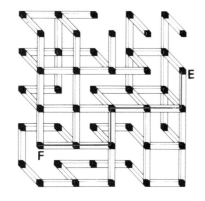

E to F = 8

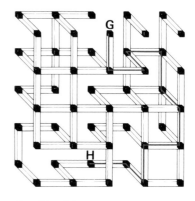

G to H = 15

Game 2

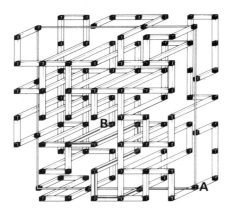

A to B = 13

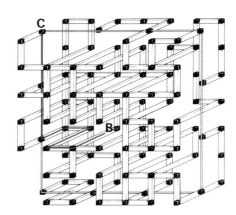

B to C = 10

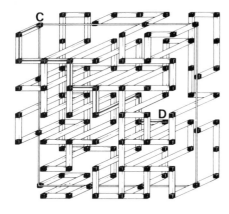

C to D = 13

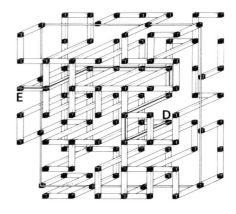

D to E = 12

COMPUTER PATTERNS PAGE 48-49

The growing screen pattern is revealed below. If the rules are not followed strictly, however, different patterns result.

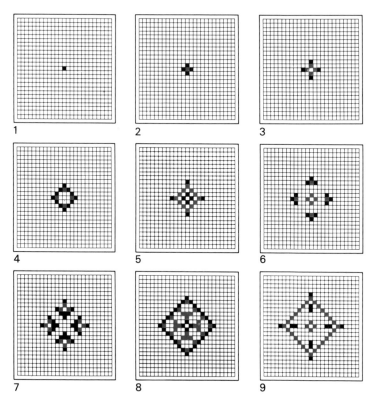

1 2 3

4 5 6

7 8 9

10

11

THE PATTERNS EXPLAINED
It's very easy, when working out these patterns, to reinterpret the rules slightly to reach what you think the next stage *ought* to be. If the patterns you have created differ from the ones shown here, this could be the reason, so read the rules again carefully.

The pattern is generated and transformed as cells change color and as new cells are added. Bear in mind that:
a. New cells *cannot* grow if the blank they would grow in is touched by existing cells on more than one side, even if the existing touching cells are pale blue and so will disappear at the instant of the new cell's birth.
b. A game starts with an 'initial configuration'. In the illustrated game this is a single, central dark blue cell. It could be any number of cells, however, in any pattern in any part of the screen.

COMPUTER PATTERNS

Once you know the rules off by heart, such growth patterns can become almost addictive in their fascination: it becomes difficult not to want to 'just see what the next pattern looks like', every sheet of squared paper in the house is quickly occupied by crystallate designs, and enthusiasts have been known to stay up late at night cursing as black and blue pens gradually run dry. The simplicity of a single set of rules applied strictly and logically over and over is almost hypnotic – and some of the results are beautiful, especially as the designs get bigger and more complex. (I can personally recommend stages 12, 13 (shown below), 17, 21, 24, 25 and *every* stage thereafter to anyone who has the patience.)

Alternatively, if the rules are changed slightly – for instance, if growth occurs only from 'second generation' (pale blue) squares – different growth patterns immediately emerge. In every case, for success the rules must be precisely defined (and understood) and rigidly adhered to. Another interesting variation is to start from a different, more complex, initial configuration (such as a bilaterally symmetrical pattern or even an asymmetrical one) or configurations – two at different corners, for example.

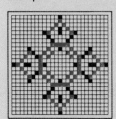

Pattern 13

ACKNOWLEDGEMENTS

Eddison/Sadd Editions would like to acknowledge the assistance and cooperation received from Clark Robinson Limited during the production of this book.

Creative Director: Nick Eddison
Art Director: Gill Della Casa
Designer: Amanda Barlow

Editorial Director: Ian Jackson
Project Editor: Hal Robinson
Copywriter: Michael Darton
Proofreader: Christine Moffat

Artists:
Keith Duran (represented by Linden Artists) 12-13, 16-17
Andrew Farmer 8-9, 24-25, 32-33, 36-37, 40-41, 42-43, 44-45
Mick Gillah 18-19, 28-29, 34-35
Kuo Kang Chen 6-7, 10-11, 20-21, 22-23, 26-27, 46-47
Larry Rostant (represented by Artists Partners) 14-15, 30-31, 38-39, 48-49
Solutions artwork:
Anthony Duke and Dave Sexton 50-63

THE FINAL SOLUTION – COVER PUZZLE

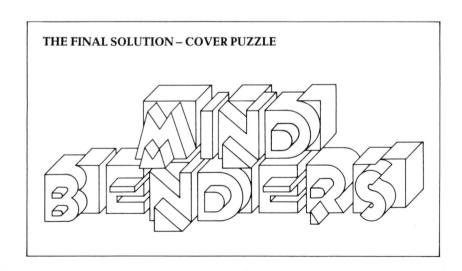